Stephanie Hillberry

THE JESUS INTERRUPTION

*Embracing My True Identity
in the Messiness of Momhood*

52 DEVOTIONS

JESUS-CENTERED DEVOTIONS

JESUS-CENTERED DEVOTIONS

The Jesus Interruption

Embracing My True Identity in the Messiness of Momhood

"I'm Getting Back on Track With Jesus…"

"I'm doing it this time!" you declare. "I've really put my relationship with Jesus on the back burner since becoming a mom, and it's time to change my priorities. What I need is a regular quiet time."

Thus the planning begins. You know you'll have to get up early, so you set your alarm and get the coffeemaker ready. In order to not be a zombie who stares off into space every morning, you'll need a new Bible study and prayer journal to stay focused. You even pick out a scented candle and worship music to set the mood.

"This is going to be great!" you say. And at first it is. Until about day five when you're exhausted and convinced you're doing something wrong.

You're *supposed* to be inspired by the Bible…but keep reading the same three sentences again and again.

You're *supposed* to be praying for other people…but can barely stay awake long enough to pray about your own problems.

And you're *supposed* to be hearing answers from Jesus…but all you hear are your own thoughts, and they sound like this:

"In 20 minutes I'll need to wake up the kids. I wonder if Kate is coming down with a cold. She felt warm last night. If she's fine, then we'll head out to the store after I drop the older kids at school. But first there's breakfast. Nick's getting so weird about eggs lately. Maybe I could try pancakes? But wait—I think I'm out of batter mix. And syrup…"

Seriously? Lamest. Quiet time. Ever.

"Dear Jesus, I'll talk to you again in maybe 15 years. Sincerely, me."

Messy Can Be Sacred, Too

If you can relate even a little to this scenario, this book is for you. Because let's just say the thing that needs to be said: Moms can't afford for their relationship with Jesus to be precious and protected. Frankly y'all don't have the time.

The good news is that quiet dawns and candlelight don't have a monopoly on sacredness. Messy can be sacred, too. Childbirth, for instance—that bloody, screaming, messy chaos that started your motherhood in the first place—is sacred. And so is the constant racket that's now your daily life.

As it turns out, our Savior (the one we oddly picture wearing serene white) is perfectly willing to roll up his sleeves and get into it beside you. In fact, maybe you should start picturing his heavenly white frock smeared with sticky grime because he's happy to interrupt your messy, chaotic days with surprising moments of sacredness. These moments are "Jesus interruptions," and they have as much power to transform your heart and life as candlelit quiet times. I promise.

So turn the page and start expecting Jesus to talk to you, to meet with you, to capture your heart and mind on the go. Invite him to break into your day at surprising times. Because when you welcome more Jesus interruptions into your day, you'll find that he's been there all along.

THE JESUS INTERRUPTION

How to Use This Devotional

Turn the page to the first devotion. Read. Repeat. (Just kidding. Though technically true, here are a few more notes...)

52 Devotions

This book includes 52 devotions—one for every week of the year. Yes, you can read ahead if you're an overachiever. Or you can spread them out over the next 15 years. Just do what's in your heart. This isn't momschool; there's no judgment.

52 Micro Quiet Times

In addition to the devotions are prompts for your daily life. These are designed to center your thoughts on Jesus in the midst of your real life. Think of them as micro quiet times.

24 Day-in-a-Mom's-Life Prayers

Sandwiched in the middle of the book are 24 Day-in-a-Mom's-Life prayers, plus ideas for your own prayers. These can come in handy if...say...you hit a wall at 4:02 p.m. and *need some Jesus now!* Open the book to the middle, find 4 p.m., and say hello to Jesus.

Journal Spaces

Finally, there are spaces for journaling sprinkled throughout. Use them to help you remember what Jesus is saying to you in the midst of your messy life.

And speaking of what Jesus is saying…

A Word About Hearing Jesus' Voice

This book refers a lot to hearing Jesus. It asks you to pray to him and then listen to what he says. Depending on your current relationship with Jesus, this listening may be like chatting with a friend or like awkwardly talking to a wall.

If you're more of the awkward-wall-talker type, take a deep breath and relax. Hearing Jesus' voice isn't as mystical and elusive as it sounds. In fact, you're already hearing from him (see Devotion 1). To hear him even more clearly, here are a few tips:

Before listening, ask Jesus to silence your own voice. You can even say out loud, "In Jesus' name, I claim God's authority over my thoughts." Then trust that the things you hear next will be from him.

Start small by asking for answers to simple prayers (vs. BIG, life-changing, I-can't-screw-this-up prayers). For instance, before graduating to "Should I change careers?" practice listening for his guidance as you set goals for the week.

Let peace guide you. If you feel uneasy about what you're hearing, keep praying. Jesus' words—even his challenging and convicting words—come with a sense of peace.

Look for confirmation about what you hear.

Confirmations often come through opening (or closing) doors, the words of someone else, or Bible verses.

Keep a journal and write down what you're hearing. This helps you distinguish your thoughts from Jesus' voice, and it helps you remember what he's saying to you.

Don't be afraid to make a mistake. Take a little leap of faith that you are hearing Jesus, and trust that if you get off track, he can lead you back.

week one

**I know it doesn't always seem like it,
but you hear Jesus. Promise.**

Some days it feels like the only thing you're listening to is the demanding drumbeat of motherhood set on repeat. Whether it's a toddler at your ankles or a steady chime of incoming texts from a high-maintenance teen, the rhythm sounds something like this:

Mom. Mom. Mom. Mom. Mom. MOM, MOMMMMMMM...

(Repeat 500 times.)

It's difficult to hear your *own* thoughts above this racket, much less the insightful voice of Jesus. His clarity, direction, and reassurance all seem muffled, like background noise you can't quite make out. This experience can lead you to believe something false, which is that you're not hearing from him.

But you *are* hearing Jesus. All day. For instance, that seemingly random thought you had about someone that prompted a spontaneous prayer—that's his voice nudging you. The sudden insight you had about why your kid was acting out—that's him. That rare moment of self-control you felt when you held your tongue instead of interfering—that's him.

Jesus is always there, speaking to you and guiding you. You're tuned into his drumbeat because it comes directly from his Spirit within you. Ask Jesus to help you recognize his voice even more, and thank him for speaking to you today.

For more, read John 10:27-28.

"My sheep listen to my voice; I know them, and they follow me. I give them eternal life, and they will never perish. No one can snatch them away from me" (JOHN 10:27-28).

THE JESUS INTERRUPTION
Have a Micro Quiet Time

Remember that drawing close to Jesus doesn't require a dedicated quiet time. This week, every time you're waiting for something (a stoplight to turn green, your computer to reboot, a doctor's appointment), take that small window of time to say hi to Jesus. Tell him how you're feeling or what you're thinking about, and then listen to what he's thinking and feeling. Repeat all week.

♥

week two

**Stop asking for energy to tackle
tomorrow's problems.**

Mom-worry is like an itch you can't quite scratch. The "what ifs" are always tickling the back of your mind. What if I lose my job? What if I get into an accident? What if I forget to remind my son about that assignment next month? What if we miss the deadline for dance class? What if…

On the surface, investing time troubleshooting what ifs can seem like prudence. Planning for contingencies means they can't catch you off-guard, right?

The treachery of worry, though, is that it never holds up its end of the bargain. It trades today's peace in exchange for future peace, but then tomorrow comes and it never delivers. You get suckered into emotionally investing today's energy into imaginary troubles—even having imaginary conversations in your head—only to do it all over again tomorrow. It's a waste, and it robs you of today's joy.

So stop it. When you catch yourself preemptively managing tomorrow's concerns, back off. Jesus has better purposes for you today. He'd much rather you expend your energy in loving the people right in front of you or managing the problems you can actually impact right now. He's given you the wisdom and strength you need to do today's work. But he has no energy to lend you for tomorrow's concerns, so stop asking. Today is plenty to handle.

For more, read Matthew 6:34.

> *"So don't worry about tomorrow, for tomorrow will bring its own worries. Today's trouble is enough for today"*
>
> (MATTHEW 6:34).

THE JESUS INTERRUPTION
Back Away From Worry

Every time a worry enters your mind this week, immediately ask yourself if it's a concern for today or for the future. If it's a future worry, picture yourself putting your hands up and backing away from the worry. Do this as many times as you need to.

week three

Stop overcomplicating purpose.

He may have just spilled the last bit of milk onto the floor or left his shoes at the foot of the stairs in a precarious booby trap or forgotten that practice ended at 4:00 instead of 6:00 (oops!), but somehow you know that beneath the hiccups and misses, your child was created for a purpose. And someday that purpose will reach people in need and change lives and leave a mark on the world.

Because you believe so strongly in this purpose, you really want to make sure that your child doesn't miss it. You can't bear the thought of him getting off track or pulled into things that don't really matter. So, like a mom, you want to *get involved*. Maybe sign him up for a class or get him to read a book or send him on a trip or something.

Here's the deal: Don't overcomplicate the process. The truth is that all of us share the same purpose, which is to love Jesus with our whole hearts and to love our neighbors. The easiest thing you can do is to live this purpose yourself. Your child will follow you. And together you'll leave a mark on the world.

For more, read 1 Corinthians 3:8 and Philippians 1:27.

"The one who plants and the one who waters work together with the same purpose. And both will be rewarded for their own hard work" (1 CORINTHIANS 3:8).

THE JESUS INTERRUPTION
Share Your Purpose

You and your child share the same purpose: to love God and love others. Together this week, identify one person each that you can show extra love to. Then share what happened.

week four

Hard stuff really does have a silver lining.

You just don't get it. You're a parent, and if you could, you'd move mountains to protect your child from painful things. You hate to see her hurting. From slivers in her fingers to breakups with her first crush, her pain is your pain. You know that hard things make her stronger, but all things being equal, you'd prefer for her to skip over hard things entirely. For that matter, you'd prefer to skip them, too.

So why, why doesn't God feel the same way? Given the opportunity (um—which he has, obviously), why doesn't he protect his children from pain? Children like you and your child?

We don't especially love the answer. "In this life you'll have troubles," Jesus said, and then painfully died on the cross God led him to. Ever since Adam and Eve, pain has been part of the deal, and if God didn't spare his own Son, he will not spare us.

The silver lining in all this suffering is the other half of what Jesus said, which is that he overcomes pain, death, darkness, and sin. Through him we overcome as well. Overcoming is not nearly as appealing as skipping the pain in the first place, but that's only because we don't have the full picture, and because we're still learning to grasp the unfathomable love Jesus has for us. Trusting this love is a great risk, and the path leads us through some dark places, but the reward is eternity. Hang in there. The prize is worth the cost.

For more, read John 16:33.

> *"I have told you all this so that you may*
> *have peace in me. Here on earth you will*
> *have many trials and sorrows. But take*
> *heart, because I have overcome the world"*
> (JOHN 16:33).

THE JESUS INTERRUPTION
In-Your-Face Reminder

Ask Jesus to give you a word to focus on this week, and write it in the space below. Then copy it to a spot you'll see often, like on your bathroom mirror in erase-able marker or scribbled on a sticky note on the fridge or on your steering wheel.

_____

_____

_____

_____

_____

week five

It's okay to be boldly needy.

Admit it: Neediness can be irritating. Which is why feeling needy yourself is especially annoying. You're the one who *meets* needs; you can't afford to *have* them, too.

Maybe this is why you're so timid when you pray, hedging your bets by asking for big things while preparing your heart to be disappointed. Why do you do this? Jesus has given you the privilege of boldly approaching God with your requests. God's answers will not always be what you want, or as clear as you'd like, but he *will* answer, and he will not scorn your request.

God is never annoyed by your neediness. In fact, rather than viewing your needs as a burden, he sees them as an opportunity to give generously, which is his nature. So don't be timid about your neediness. Come confidently with it. You'll be welcomed.

For more, read Hebrews 4:16.

"So let us come boldly to the throne of our gracious God. There we will receive his mercy, and we will find grace to help us when we need it most" (HEBREWS 4:16).

THE JESUS INTERRUPTION
Embrace Your Neediness

Neediness feels awkward, but Jesus invites it. So practice getting comfortable with your neediness this week by sharing a need on social media or with a friend, and then asking for help.

How Has Jesus Interrupted You Lately?

Writing things down helps us see how much we're growing, so spend 60 seconds listing every connection, interruption, insight, and word that you've shared with Jesus recently.

_____

_____

_____

_____

_____

_____

_____

_____

_____

_____

_____

_____

_____

week six

**Your greatest temptation is
not what you think.**

Jesus knows the things that tempt you. Forget chocolate cake. Forget Netflix binges. Forget the clearance rack at the department store. These are easy temptations—light, passing burdens.

Here's what *really* tempts you—the thing that's so enticing, so alluring, that you don't even recognize it when you're in its snare.

It's CONTROL.

If you could Just. Have. A. Little. More. Just a teensy bit extra would make you feel calmer, more organized, more put together. You'd be able to plan, to stay ahead of the chaos. More control would help you be a better mom—more reliable and trustworthy.

And so you turn to the tactics of control, including time management, command centers, routines, rules. You plan, you schedule, you coordinate contingencies. And on the outside, it all looks excellent and praiseworthy. Because what's admired today is a woman who takes control of her life.

But that's not Jesus' kind of woman. He wants a dependent woman. A woman who's not *out of control* exactly, but who *surrenders control*. She lets him guide her step by step, trusting him instead of her own plans and agendas.

Be *that* kind of woman. Resist the temptation to take control of your life; do the unexpected thing by giving it up instead. He promises that when you lose it, you'll find it.

For more, read John 14:1.

> *"Don't let your hearts be troubled. Trust in God, and trust also in me"* (JOHN 14:1).

THE JESUS INTERRUPTION
Let Jesus Drive
Do the unexpected today. Get into your car and ask Jesus to direct you to your destination. At each intersection give him an opportunity to say which way to go. See where he takes you.

week seven

**So this is a little awkward,
but your child is sinful.**

This is a weird way to start a devotion, right? I mean, of course you know that your child is sinful. Not serial killer sinful—just garden variety, I-want-what-I-want-NOW sinful. He's sinful like you—like everybody.

This sinfulness directly contradicts a pernicious little lie that many parents believe. The lie is that children are born as beautiful blank slates. Entrusted into your care, this baby will either drift to the good or bad side of the dividing line, depending on how you raise him. Each decision you make marks up his slate for light or dark.

No pressure, right?

Don't buy into it. Your kid was never a blank slate. He was born into sin and from day one was destined to be a fatally flawed combination of light and dark. This bad news sounds harsh, except for two things.

First, you're off the hook. Though incredibly valuable, your parenting doesn't have the power to save your child, so don't shoulder that burden. Furthermore, you didn't make him sinful. He was born that way, and no amount of parenting can change that.

Second, Jesus does save, totally and completely. He's willing and able to redeem all sins, including your child's. Only he has the power to turn a dark, sinful slate into a blank one. You can trust him to do it for your kid.

For more, read Romans 3:23.

> *"For everyone has sinned; we all fall short of God's glorious standard"* (ROMANS 3:23).

THE JESUS INTERRUPTION
Focus on Your Kid's Identity in Jesus

Look at a picture of your child and ask Jesus to put one word into your mind for her today. Make a note of what you hear, and pray over her, using that word throughout the week.

week eight

It's time to evict your inner mean girl
and her cousins.

We all have one, including you. It's that critical, sneering voice we hear in our head. She's a mean girl, shaming us for saying things we regret, poking at our insecurities, starting sentences with, "You know—you really *should*..." and constantly reminding us of our mistakes.

Yes, *that* mean girl.

Let's send her an eviction notice, shall we? Because honestly—she makes for horrible company. And let's get rid of her irritating cousins—Distraction, Forgetfulness, and Anxiety—too. They're much too fond of meddling in our thoughts, don't you think?

Jesus is ready and willing to help you remove this mean girl and her cousins. His presence is powerful enough to drown them out with his truthful words. Of course this doesn't happen overnight (they're persistent and disinclined to cooperate), but when you draw closer to him, he promises that your thoughts can increasingly become his thoughts. So start today. Ask Jesus to interrupt, talk over, and generally be rude to your mean thoughts, and practice listening to his voice instead.

For more, read 2 Corinthians 10:5.

"We destroy every proud obstacle that keeps people from knowing God. We capture their rebellious thoughts and teach them to obey Christ" (2 CORINTHIANS 10:5).

THE JESUS INTERRUPTION
Turn Off Comparison
Turn off social media for a day (or more) this week, and take a break from the temptation to compare yourself with others. Spend the time enjoying something you like, and invite Jesus to join you.

week nine

You can let go. You really can.

Roller coasters. Spiders. *Clowns*. These are things that put fear into the hearts of many. Also, small, tight spaces and soaring heights. Or needles or cancer or war.

As a mom, something else scares you. Something that makes you shake your head and say, "No, I can't do it. I can't face it. I. Just. Can't. Even."

This is the fear of letting go.

The hard truth of motherhood is that you pour yourself into these tiny creatures until they one day grow up and become full-sized humans. AND THEN THEY LEAVE YOU. And though you know this is the deal from the very beginning, it still scares you. Because eventually they'll be out there on their own. Free to make mistakes and get hurt and choose poorly. Free to do good stuff, too, though that's not what you're afraid of.

You're already getting a taste of this letting go. Her first few steps. Her first day of school. Her first car. Her first prom. It never stops.

If there's one good thing about letting go, it's that you free up your heart to trust and love Jesus more, remembering that you were made for one thing first, and it isn't parenting. This doesn't seem like such a good thing when your mom heart is squeezed tight, but the paradox of letting go in Jesus' kingdom is that those who lose will find again.

For more, read Luke 17:33.

> "If you cling to your life, you will lose it,
>
> and if you let your life go, you will save it"
>
> (LUKE 17:33).

THE JESUS INTERRUPTION
Let Go of Your Plans

Using the space below, write your agenda for tomorrow. Then cross everything off and ask Jesus to create a new agenda for you. Write down what you hear him say.

_____

_____

_____

_____

_____

_____

_____

week ten

You're not the only one who loves your kid unconditionally.

Suddenly it clicked. All your life you'd heard of love and dreamed of love and felt love. But when you became a mom, you understood love in an entirely new way. "Ah," you said. "*Now* I get it." Now you know what they mean about a love that can't be defeated by mistakes or hurt or neglect.

Unconditional love.

You feel that no one can love your child as fiercely as you do. Except there is another, and his love was fierce enough to lead him to death. No matter what your child does, Jesus feels the same way about him that you do. Whether he understands Jesus' love, or accepts it, it's covering him.

Let this reassurance of love comfort your heart. Trust that Jesus' love will produce rich and wonderful things in your child's life. Pray today that your child will feel and trust and accept this love and walk under its cover every day.

For more, read Ephesians 3:17-18.

"Then Christ will make his home in your hearts as you trust in him. Your roots will grow down into God's love and keep you strong. And may you have the power to understand, as all God's people should, how wide, how long, how high, and how deep his love is" (EPHESIANS 3:17-18).

THE JESUS INTERRUPTION
Pay Ridiculous Attention to Your Kid

Make a decision to pay really close attention to your kid this week, looking for good things he's doing that might normally go unnoticed. Watch for things like showing extra patience or demonstrating a strong work ethic, or suppressing a complaint or argument. If you see something like this, call it out casually, telling him that you notice what he's doing and that you're proud of him.

How Has Jesus Interrupted You Lately?
Writing things down helps us see how much we're growing, so spend 60 seconds listing every connection, interruption, insight, and word that you've shared with Jesus recently.

_____

_____

_____

_____

_____

_____

_____

_____

_____

_____

_____

_____

_____

week eleven

**Cheers to chucking rules
and faux standards!**

"No, don't touch that!"

"Yes, you may stay over at Ryan's house, but no, you may not go to the R-rated movie together."

"No, you may not have Red Vines for dinner, but yes, you can have these potatoes I made."

"No, you may not play one more game. Yes, I know it will take five minutes, but the answer is still no."

Being a mom means setting A LOT of rules. *Constantly.* Rules about friends, about media, about dating. Rules about bedtime and screen time and playtime.

As if all these mom rules aren't enough, you set almost as many for yourself to follow. No snacks after 7 p.m. No TV until the dishes are done. No new clothes until you save more money. No reward until you lose 10 pounds.

Of course rules are valuable—they help us choose what's good for us and resist what harms us. But many of our rules promise good only to deliver guilt and shame instead.

Jesus wants to do two things for you when it comes to rule-setting. First, he wants to set you free from rules that bind you by welcoming and accepting you as you are. This includes any sloppy, disorganized, unmotivated, undisciplined, overweight, and unattractive parts. This means that *you don't have to work so hard!* Consider yourself cordially invited to chuck those false standards and accept grace instead.

I mean it. Chuck them. Like right now.

The second thing Jesus wants to do is invite himself

into your daily life. He's genuinely interested in helping you make choices and has good ideas about what's healthy for you. So the next time you find yourself setting a new rule, pause and ask him what he has to say about it. His answer might surprise you.

For more, read John 8:34-36 and Colossians 2:20-23.

"So if the Son sets you free, you are truly free" (JOHN 8:36).

THE JESUS INTERRUPTION
Red or Green?

Before starting a new self-improvement program (diet, time-management, decluttering), pause to examine your motives and ask Jesus to share his input. Let him alert you if shame, hurt, or perfectionism is driving your plans instead of his direction, or if you're in danger of biting off more than you can chew. Then wait for his peace before moving forward.

week twelve

**On getting a bigger,
better perspective**

"I just didn't expect the time to go by so fast."

Motherhood is a blink. A breath, and then they're grown. A flashing string of summers and holidays, of games and concerts and movie nights, filling up the pages of scrapbooks and digital albums. You frantically capture as many moments as you can, hoping somehow to slow down time.

Each moment is precious, and you have only one life.

If your heart is racing, here's a reminder to help slow it down: Yes, you have only one life, but you were made for eternity. These seasons and years blurring by are just a fraction of what Jesus has planned for you and those he loves.

The passage of time can seem relentless, consuming your purpose and heart with each passing day. But as hard as it is to fathom, this life is just a beginning.

Jesus knew we would have a hard time with this perspective, which is why he talked about eternity so frequently, reminding us that this earth is not our home. The sacrificial love you offer your kid will not erode with time. It's eternal. The spirit of your kid is eternal. Love is eternal.

So when everything feels fragile and temporary, remember that you belong to something that's solid and everlasting. Jesus' kingdom will last forever, and you're a part of it.

For more, read Colossians 3:2.

"Think about the things of heaven, not the things of earth" (COLOSSIANS 3:2).

THE JESUS INTERRUPTION

Focus on Heaven

This week, each time you have a thought that relates to this temporary life, immediately counter it with a thought about heaven. For example, a thought like "I wish my kid would stop growing up so fast" could be followed by "In heaven, no one gets older, and we get to be together forever."

week thirteen

Here's an inconvenient truth
about suffering.

Let's talk about something that's unpopular, starting with something that's really popular, namely comfort, happiness, and success. According to books, magazines, blogs, and movies, being a mom is only a fraction of your potential. "Don't limit yourself," they say. "You deserve to have it all."

This message is like candy. It tastes sweet and makes you feel good. It also goes down *much* easier than Jesus' message, which is an invitation to suffer with him. (Imagine *that* headline on a glossy magazine cover.)

Whereas the popular message has all the very best marketers—shiny celebrity spokespeople living enviable lives—Jesus had 12 dusty dudes from two centuries ago who built up a fan base and then died sacrificially.

It's easy to see why we'd gravitate toward the popular crowd, right?

But don't be lured by sweet candy that only delivers empty calories. Following Jesus and sharing in his suffering sounds like eating dirt, but it's really honey in disguise. Jesus compared it to a pearl buried in a field; in fact, it's worth everything.

Regardless of what magazines and blogs say, to pour out your life for a Savior and King is far better than to build yourself up into a false queen. Your true inheritance is richer and more rewarding than the glitz the world promises. Keep your eye on the prize. His name is Jesus.

For more, read Romans 8:17.

"And since we are his children, we are his heirs. In fact, together with Christ we are heirs of God's glory. But if we are to share his glory, we must also share his suffering" (ROMANS 8:17).

THE JESUS INTERRUPTION
Thank Jesus for Hard Things

Scroll back through your social media feed from the past few months. Think about all of the challenging things you were experiencing in the background when you published those posts. Thank Jesus for how he uses trials and sacrifice to draw you closer to him. Then think about people you know who are in the midst of hard times. Spend a minute praying for them.

week fourteen

You're invited to toss out benchmarks.

Report cards. Wellness visits. Height and weight charts. From the moment you have children, other people start trying to measure them. Are they tall enough? Do they weigh enough? (And then later, do they weigh too much?) Are they talking on time and writing on time and playing well with others?

When they get older, the metrics get more intense. How's their test performance? Are they set up for success in college? Do they have special skills that set them apart from the other kids, things that make them stand out?

It's easy to be anxious about these benchmarks and measurements. Not only do you feel like they're a judgment on your value as a parent, but you worry that the world won't see your child for who she is.

Regardless of these benchmarks, your child's value is measured by exactly one thing: Jesus. Your kid doesn't have anything to prove. She's liberated from false standards, and you're liberated with her.

For more, read Philippians 3:8-9.

"Yes, everything else is worthless when compared with the infinite value of knowing Christ Jesus my Lord. For his sake I have discarded everything else, counting it all as garbage, so that I could gain Christ and become one with him" (PHILIPPIANS 3:8-9).

THE JESUS INTERRUPTION
Take a Step Back

Warning: This challenge is hard. This week, intentionally decide *not* to meet a need or come to your child's rescue. Choose something he can wait a little longer for, can easily go without, or can figure out himself. Each time you feel that tug in your heart to swoop in, remember that Jesus is your child's ultimate Savior and that he's taking full responsibility for his job.

week fifteen

When the whole world is conspiring against you, do this.

You hit the red light at exactly the wrong time. And then a train came. *Great.*

You opened the car door to grab the grocery bag just as the bottom ripped open and the eggs fell out. On the driveway. *Super.*

You finally got all the kids to bed and finished up the dishes and had just set your feet on the sofa when the smoke alarm went off. For no reason whatsoever. Six times in a row. *Best. Night. Ever.*

There are days—*oh, there are days*—when it seems like everything is against you. Days when big and small things go wrong. Days when raining becomes pouring and you're left without an umbrella. These days can be funny in retrospect, but when you're in the midst of them, they're no laughing matter. They make you feel defeated, alone, and exhausted.

So here's what you do when you're in the middle of one of those days: You believe that Jesus is for you (which is true even if it doesn't feel like it) and that he has a new beginning for you, starting NOW. And then you wait on his peace and strength until you feel it. You may have to repeat this process *every minute of the day* until you fall asleep, but so be it. He'll deliver you from these trials, but he might do it one minute at a time. Take a deep breath, relax, and lean on him. A better day is coming.

For more, read Romans 8:31-32.

"What shall we say about such wonderful things as these? If God is for us, who can ever be against us?" (ROMANS 8:31).

THE JESUS INTERRUPTION
Hit the Reset Button
Each time you hit a rough patch this week, repeat the following mantra: "Jesus is starting a new thing NOW," and then wait for his help. Keep repeating throughout the day as needed, remembering that Jesus is for you when things seem against you.

How Has Jesus Interrupted You Lately?

Writing things down helps us see how much we're growing, so spend 60 seconds listing every connection, interruption, insight, and word that you've shared with Jesus recently.

---

week sixteen

Upgrade who you see in the mirror.

Pretend with me that you're in an alternate universe. This universe is identical to the one you live in now except for one major difference: The mirrors in the dressing room make you look *better*. (Cue the singing angels.)

That's right—you look good. Not chubby and pasty with the dark, droopy eyelids of an unflattering cartoon villain, but *good*. Your smile is brighter, your eyes twinkle, your skin is dewy. You even seem funnier and more gracious and more intelligent.

This fantasy is actually not a fantasy at all. This is what Jesus does: He reflects our true image back to us. Unlike the distorted fun-house mirrors we're used to, warped by sin and lies and baggage from our past, Jesus' mirror shows the best version of us—the version he sees, the version he died for.

This genuine reflection is a gift with the power to transform how we see ourselves. And because we follow Jesus, we can be like his mirror to others, too, reflecting back to them who they truly are. This reflection offers hope, and Jesus' love makes it real. So pray today about becoming Jesus' mirror to those around you, starting now.

For more, read 2 Corinthians 3:18.

"So all of us who have had that veil removed can see and reflect the glory of the Lord. And the Lord—who is the Spirit—makes us more and more like him as we are changed into his glorious image"

(2 CORINTHIANS 3:18).

THE JESUS INTERRUPTION
See a New Thing
Every time you get dressed this week, remind yourself that you're a new creation with Jesus—the old you is being replaced by a new thing Jesus is doing *today*. Thank him for this new thing, and then walk away from the mirror in anticipation.

week seventeen

Go ahead—shake off that pesky peer pressure.

Remember when peer pressure was an adolescent thing? Like when you were 12 and obsessed with what people thought of your outfit and what they were saying behind your back?

Thank goodness you outgrew that, right? You're a fully grown person now with your own identity, *thank you very much*. Peer pressure doesn't exist in your world.

Except does it ever so slightly feel like you're still being pressured? Like the opinions of other moms are important, and you're worried about what they might be saying behind your back?

In this era of information (thank you, Internet), there are so many opinions and philosophies about how to raise kids, each vying for the opportunity to shape your identity. Like a tug-of-war, you feel the tension between what's in your heart and what everyone else is doing.

This tension is normal. But it doesn't have to drive you crazy or cause you to revert to an awkward adolescent girl. Jesus has something better for you than peer pressure. *He* wants to be the one guiding and influencing you. And though he might challenge you, he doesn't manipulate you. So look for peace and relief in your heart when you come to a decision (not a tight pressure in your chest, which is how peer pressure feels), because that relief is him. He's the peer you want to listen to first.

For more, read 1 Corinthians 10:31 and Colossians 2:8-10.

> *"So whether you eat or drink, or whatever you do, do it all for the glory of God"*
>
> (1 CORINTHIANS 10:31).

THE JESUS INTERRUPTION
See What Sticks Out

The next time you hop onto social media or the Internet, pray for Jesus to bring something or someone to your attention. Then see what sticks out to you. Once you find it, dig deeper in prayer and follow his lead.

week eighteen

Here's an unlikely prayer tutor.

THE JESUS INTERRUPTION

Kids are good at a lot of things. Bedtime stalling tactics. Annoying siblings in under three seconds. Saying wildly imaginative things that make people laugh, or poignantly wise things that make people ponder.

They're also good at something you might be overlooking: hearing the voice of Jesus.

Perhaps you're under the impression that hearing Jesus' voice is an adult thing—a kind of skill people learn through practice and spiritual discipline. This is a false impression. In truth, kids can hear Jesus in surprising and powerful ways, seeing things with a simple spiritual clarity that's closer to truth than our cloudy, grown-up way of seeing things.

And because they have the ability to approach prayer playfully, kids can even teach us how to lighten up and relate to a Savior who is himself playful. So the next time you're ready to pray together, ask Jesus a question, and then let your kids tell you what they hear. The answer may spark the best truth you encounter all day.

For more, read Matthew 11:25 and 19:14.

> *"Jesus prayed this prayer: 'O Father, Lord of heaven and earth, thank you for hiding these things from those who think themselves wise and clever, and for revealing them to the childlike'"* (Matthew 11:25).

THE JESUS INTERRUPTION
Make Childlike Assumptions

Today, ask Jesus to help you pay close attention to how your child's faith works. For instance, take note of assumptions he makes easily ("Of course I'll be fed!"). With every new observation, ask Jesus to strengthen your faith by showing you childlike assumptions you can make, too.

week nineteen

Your words bring life.

You there, with the messy top knot on your head and a stain on your T-shirt. Yeah, you. I want you to know that you're a bearer of light and life disguised in the everyday, slightly disheveled attire of a mom.

You bear life not just from your womb or your heart, but from your tongue, too. Your words have the power to shape a new generation with truth. Your spoken words sharpen character. Your affirmations heal.

As an ambassador of Jesus, you are his spokesperson to the world. This includes your child, but also friends, family members, neighbors, and strangers at the store. You have a rare gift to offer, which is the ability to see others as Jesus sees them and then share that good news with them. Don't underestimate the impact these words have. Because they're from God, they go forward to complete his mission of redemption and transformation. This is pretty awesome for…say…an average Tuesday conversation in yoga pants, right?

So the next time you're in the company of others, ask Jesus to give you a word or phrase to weave into the conversation. Then thank him for his truth, and wait to see how it grows.

For more, read 2 Corinthians 5:20.

"So we are Christ's ambassadors; God is making his appeal through us. We speak for Christ when we plead, 'Come back to God!'"

(2 CORINTHIANS 5:20).

THE JESUS INTERRUPTION
A Scented Reminder

Treat yourself to a nice scented soap or fragrance this week. Every time you smell it, remember that your words bring the fragrance of life to those around you. Use the scent as a way to remind you to speak from the heart.

J.

week twenty

Truth looks a lot like you.

The world is full of broken people: the husband who cheated, the friend who can never see her role in the problem, the family member with an addiction. These people are missing a vital ingredient in their lives: truth. You know this because truth sets people free, and they're not free.

Many people today claim to have truth, and yet they go their own way, pursuing their desires and interests. But you're different because you know what *real* truth looks like. It's not a set of rules or lines drawn in the sand. Truth is washing the feet of others. Truth is embracing the outcast. Truth is seeing beneath people's exteriors and into their hearts. Truth is sacrificial. Truth is challenging. Truth is service.

In other words, truth looks a lot like you.

Turns out, all this sacrificial love you're offering in your daily life has been training you in the practice of truth-telling. This is good news because the world is in great need, and you are Jesus' ambassador. You can't set broken people free—that's Jesus' job—but you can bring them truth. By doing so, you bring Jesus with you. He does the rest.

For more, read 1 Timothy 3:15 and John 8:32.

> *"And you will know the truth, and the truth will set you free"* (JOHN 8:32).

THE JESUS INTERRUPTION
Invite Jesus to Be Your Shadow

Throughout your day, picture Jesus shadowing you as you interact with others. Envision him interacting with them. Pay attention to what he says and does. Then try to copy. What happens?

How Has Jesus Interrupted You Lately?

Writing things down helps us see how much we're growing, so spend 60 seconds listing every connection, interruption, insight, and word that you've shared with Jesus recently.

_____

_____

_____

_____

_____

_____

_____

_____

_____

_____

_____

_____

week
twenty-one

When it comes to what really matters, you're ahead of the curve.

THE JESUS INTERRUPTION

If ever there was a crucial message for Jesus-followers that moms get, it's laying down your life for others. This is a particularly difficult thing to do, but moms are ahead of the curve, setting an example for others.

So cheers to you! Every day you're sacrificing your needs and wants for the well-being of others. You're building others up, making them stand tall in truth. Even when you feel empty, you dig deep and give more. Then you go to bed and do it all over again the next day.

This sacrificial lifestyle isn't very popular with the who's who. They think we need to care for ourselves first. They're concerned about being taken advantage of, of burning out, of becoming a doormat. But you don't have to worry about that nonsense, because you have Jesus looking out for you and caring for you. This act of laying down your life for others is so dear to his heart that he died, literally, to share it. He's committed to lifting you up as you follow in his footsteps, and he will give you everything you need to be faithful today.

For more, read Philippians 2:17.

"I will rejoice even if I lose my life, pouring it out like a liquid offering to God"

(PHILIPPIANS 2:17).

THE JESUS INTERRUPTION
Circle Jesus' Priorities

Got five minutes? Sit down and write down *everything* on your mind in the space provided, including things to do, worries, conversations you've had, and things you're excited about. When you're finished, ask Jesus to help you circle the things that are his priority for you. Then concentrate on those.

_____

_____

_____

_____

_____

_____

_____

_____

_____

_____

_____

week twenty-two

The secret to raising strong kids isn't what you think.

The world needs gritty kids—kids with character and determination and resilience. Kids with strength to overcome life's inevitable challenges and heartaches.

One of the mom-duties we take seriously is to help our kids be strong. But here's a twist on strength: Jesus says that it's in your child's weaknesses that he's strong. This feels like a poor bargain—we don't want our children to be weak because it increases their chances of being hurt. But the secret truth is that weakness— not strength—pulls them into the presence of Jesus, teaching them how to rely on him instead of their own efforts. This is an invaluable lesson and will get them much further in life than learning to rely on themselves.

So here's a weird prayer for you today: Ask Jesus to grow your child's weaknesses while teaching her to draw on his strength and grit instead of her own.

For more, read 2 Corinthians 12:9-10.

"I am glad to boast about my weaknesses, so that the power of Christ can work through me" (2 CORINTHIANS 12:9).

THE JESUS INTERRUPTION
Honor Weakness-Turned-to-Strength in Others

This week, search on TV, YouTube, or social media for an inspiring story of someone who has a disability or special need and has used it to bring hope to others. Talk with your family about how weakness can be more powerful than strength, and then invite Jesus to be strong in your weaknesses.

week twenty-three

Stop putting words in Jesus' mouth.

"Goodbye—I love you!"

"Goodnight—I love you. See you in the morning."

"Talk to you soon. Love you!"

As a mom, you say "I love you" countless times. You say it in the morning before work, after school, before practice, and after a performance. You say it on holidays and birthdays and Tuesdays. Even when you're not saying it with your words, your heart is saying it. I love you with this sandwich. I love you with this sport's fee (though I *really* don't love the fee). I love you with this hug and this song and this load of laundry.

All these I love you's are meant to leave a lasting imprint on the heart of your child. "Never forget," you're saying to him. "You're loved. No matter what happens, you're loved."

Giving love as a mom is natural, like breathing. Receiving love, on the other hand, is more difficult. This is a bummer because Jesus is as open and frequent with his I love you's as you are with yours. And his love comes with no strings attached. He never says, "I love you, *but…*"

"I love you, but could you change this one little thing?" "I love you, but could you try harder?" "I love you, but could you be better?"

If these conditional I love you's are the kind of love messages you're hearing from Jesus, then you're putting words in his mouth. He wants you to stop doing that. Don't edit his love because it makes you feel uncomfortable or unworthy. Love is his gift to give freely, and yours to receive.

So tonight, when you fall into bed, listen for his "I love you." And then don't add anything to it, for heaven's sake.

For more, read John 3:16.

"For this is how God loved the world: He gave his one and only Son, so that everyone who believes in him will not perish but have eternal life" (JOHN 3:16).

THE JESUS INTERRUPTION
Take a Smartphone Timeout
Choose one day this week to turn off your phone or put it out of reach for a designated period of time. (You get to choose how long, but aim for a timeframe that stretches you just a bit.) During that time, center your thoughts on Jesus. Even if they wander (which they will—that's okay), keep turning them back to him, listening to what he might say.

week twenty-four

**Remember that lonely and alone
are two different things.**

How is it that you can be surrounded all day by others and yet still feel alone? Granted, some of these days are filled with people who throw food like gorillas (toddlers) or grunt indecipherably (teenage boys). But still, let's be honest—some days of motherhood are lonely.

Part of this loneliness comes from the weight of responsibility you carry as a mom. Though you have support, at the end of the day you're accountable for your parenting decisions. No one can make your choices for you, and no one will take responsibility for them on your behalf.

In spite of this, don't let your *loneliness* convince you that you're actually *alone*. Because you're not alone. Jesus is always there, sitting beside you. In fact, if it helps you, picture him next to you right now.

Jesus wants to help carry the burden of parenting with you, giving you answers and offering comfort and energy. He's there at 3 a.m. when you're fretting. He's there when you have to make a snap parenting decision with no margin for error. He's calming your anxiety, giving you answers, and generally acting as your safety net.

And it's not just him supporting you. Other people are there, too, sent by him to help. They're there to offer advice, a listening ear, an encouraging word, and a prayer. Say yes to their support, and yes to Jesus, too. No mom is an island, including you.

(*Psst.* Now you're distracted by daydreams of being on

an island by yourself, aren't you? I'm sorry I mentioned it. This is my new ending: No mom is an abandoned concrete basketball court in the ghetto. Better? I thought so. You're welcome and goodbye.)

For more, read John 14:18 and Matthew 28:20.

"No, I will not abandon you as orphans—I will come to you" (JOHN 14:18).

THE JESUS INTERRUPTION
Remember You're Not Alone

Choose a special ring or piece of jewelry to wear this week to represent Jesus' nearness all day and night. Every time you touch it or look at it, remember that you're not alone.

24 Day-in-a-Mom's-Life Prayers

Invite Jesus into the messiness of an average day using these prayer examples and ideas.

THE JESUS INTERRUPTION

Dear Jesus,

The sun's barely up, and I'm *dragging*. My eyes won't focus; maybe it's because of the weight of the bags underneath them. So…basically I'm going to need your strength right out of the gate. As soon as I get some coffee and start functioning like a normal person, I'm going to need your help getting the crew up and ready. Okay? Let's do this.

Prayer idea for this hour: Ask Jesus for his strength for your morning routine. Then commit to taking it one hour at a time.

Hi again, Jesus. It's me—the slightly haggard one with a hint of dishevel.

It appears that we're currently in the midst of some *morning shenanigans*. Of course there was a fight over cereal because the box didn't have enough for two. And you probably witnessed that fashion meltdown in the hallway because I forgot to clean someone's favorite shirt (how *could* I?). Then we hit a smooth patch for a few minutes, and I dared to take a breath…right before the car keys disappeared for seven minutes.

Jesus, I'll never get back that time. Please, please help us make it out the door in one piece and get to our destinations safe and sound.

Prayer idea for this hour: Ask Jesus to protect your family and to open doors to follow his plans all day long.

8 A.M. TO 9 A.M.

Dear Jesus,

This is it: my only quiet time of the day. I have actual solitude for the next eleven-ish minutes as I drive. So here's my heart: I'm feeling frazzled and also a little hopeful at the same time. What about you? What's on your heart? I know we don't have long to talk, but I'm listening. Show me what this day looks like through your eyes.

Prayer idea for this hour: Find three minutes of quiet (hide in the bathroom, maybe?) and check in with Jesus. Tell him about your heart—what you're feeling, what's worrying you. Ask him for one thing he'd like you to focus on today.

9 A.M. TO 10 A.M.

Dear Jesus,

We're headed into that time of day when I get so busy with to-do's and agendas and appointments that I stop talking to you altogether. I feel bad about this—like I'm missing out on your wisdom and insight as I go through my day. Today I pray for more awareness of you. Send me reminders about your presence through my messages and lists and conversations. Give me ideas of how to keep you in the loop. And please guide my mind and hands as I get through this next hour.

Prayer idea for this hour: Ask Jesus to interrupt you throughout the morning, especially if you're busy. Listen intently for him to speak and guide you as you march through your to-do list.

10 A.M. TO 11 A.M.

Dear Jesus,

Can I just be honest and say that I don't want to do anything right now? Can't we just knock off and be unproductive? *No?* FINE. Then here's what I really need from you right now: *motivation.* I have so much on my mind and things I have to do, but I'm uninspired by all of it. Frankly, I'd rather be watching TV. By myself.

With snacks. But since that isn't an option, I need your help. Give me your focus and discipline to tackle what's in front of me and not get overwhelmed. Thank you for giving me purpose and things to do. Help me to actually want to do them.

Prayer idea for this hour: Ask Jesus to remind you of your purpose and to give you inspiration and encouragement as you continue with your day. Change your perspective based on what you hear.

11 A.M. TO NOON

Dear Jesus,

How is it possible that this day is both dragging and flying by? I don't understand these strange physics. I know I should be focusing on my to-do list, but I need to bring you some worries that have been pestering me all morning. It's about the kids. I wish they weren't struggling right now. I'm worried about Sadie's friend situation. Brian has tryouts next week, and, honestly, I don't think he's going to make the cut. What am I going to do with his disappointment? I can't stand the idea of how upset he'll be.

Here are my requests: I pray that my kids will have good, close friends. And I pray that they'll have your perfect balance of failure and success. I know that balance isn't always what I think it should be. So please help me to trust that you care about my kids as much as I do. Help me release my worries to you, and to feel more peace.

Prayer idea: Check in with Jesus with prayer requests for people he's putting on your heart. Take a short step back from your routine and follow his lead as you pray for others.

NOON TO 1 P.M.

Dear Jesus,

Thank you for this food. And for the opportunity to serve others by caring for their most basic needs EVERY SINGLE DAY UNTIL THE END OF TIME. Okay, so maybe I'm being a little sarcastic. You say it's a privilege to serve, so I want to *want* to do it. I'm not saying I'm there yet, so please help me feel less worn and resentful. Because most of the time I feel lucky. Change my heart, and thank you for providing for us.

Prayer idea for this hour: Take a minute to thank Jesus for the morning, and then do a quick heart check for any fatigue or resentment you might be feeling. Surrender these emotions by asking for his help in removing them.

1 P.M. TO 2 P.M.

Dear Jesus,

This is usually the time of day when I start feeling guilty and hard-pressed about all the stuff I didn't get done this morning. But you've been talking to me a lot lately about how my day isn't measured by how much I do, so I'm trying to relax. And have some more coffee. And take one long, deep breath as I listen to you. What should I do next? Show me the thing on my schedule that's your pick for this hour.

Prayer idea for this hour: Acknowledge any guilt, shame, or other negative feelings kicked up during the day, especially as they relate to your value. Ask Jesus to reset your attitude for the afternoon, and to remind you of what's most important.

2 P.M. TO 3 P.M.

Dear Jesus,

Confession: I'm feeling a bit peevish right now. I'm spread so thin and don't have a lot of margin for dealing with my buttons being pushed, which is why you just saw me lose my temper. But now I feel bad. I should have kept my mouth shut or shown more self-control or walked away—or something. Definitely not a shining example of grace and patience right now, that's for sure.

Thank you for forgiving me when I lose my cool. Please calm me down and give me more patience and peace. I know this stuff isn't that important in the grand scheme of things. Show me things through your perspective—it's always better and bigger than mine.

Prayer idea for this hour: Ask Jesus for extra grace and forgiveness of others, and for help removing defensiveness or irritability.

3 P.M. TO 4 P.M.

Dear Jesus,

Thank you that the afternoon is coming to an end. It couldn't have come sooner because I've officially hit a wall. My brain is pure mush, and I need a recharge. I need help to push through my to-do list and to prepare for whatever moods and shenanigans await me later this afternoon. Give me a second wind.

Prayer idea for this hour: Ask Jesus for a boost of energy as you transition into late afternoon/evening. Surrender your weariness, and ask him to fill you with strength, believing that he will.

4 P.M. TO 5 P.M.

Dear Jesus,

It's here—the dreaded witching hour. That twilight zone between the afternoon and dinner when the Earth seems to stop moving on its axis and children GO TO CRAZY TOWN. I'm not gonna lie: I feel like I might lose it. I'm right on the edge. Lord, give me patience and wisdom. Help me get over this hump.

Prayer idea for this hour: Ask Jesus to give you an extra measure of the fruits of his Spirit (love, joy, peace, patience, kindness, goodness, faithfulness, gentleness, and self-control), and to flood your home/car/ environment with peace. Also ask for wisdom about how to troubleshoot particularly hard hours of your day and redeem them for his purpose.

5 P.M. TO 6 P.M.

Dear Jesus,

It's feeding time again. Or at least prep for feeding time. I want to pause while I'm in the middle of this prep to say thank you. Sadie told me about her day, and it was so encouraging to me to see that you've answered her prayers (and mine). Thank you for caring about her faith and the small details of her life. She needed today's boost, and so did I. I'm so thankful for her. I pray that you'll send more little wins like this.

Prayer idea for this hour: Think about the good things that have happened today, and ask Jesus to open your eyes to things you may have missed. Thank him for all of them.

Dear Jesus,

The end is in sight; the wind-down is just hours away. But first I pray over this next hour: Open windows for my family to connect with each other, especially a chance for me to listen to Alex. It feels like we've been missing each other lately, so I pray for a good conversation (even if it's only for five minutes). Help me discern what's happening beneath the surface with him, and give me wisdom for what to say (and when to keep my mouth shut and just listen). I pray over our family this next hour, that in the midst of homework and chores and shows and *stuff* that we'd know how much we love each other and how much you love us. Keep us together, Jesus.

Prayer idea for this hour: Ask Jesus for special discernment as you relate to your family—for eyes to see what's *really* going on with your kids and spouse, and for good conversations.

7 P.M. TO 8 P.M.

Dear Jesus,

Okay, okay—one day I know I'll look back on these evenings with nostalgia, longing for these simple family routines, but right now I just want to cross the threshold to Glorious Grown-Up Time already. So I ask for extra patience with the kids tonight. I pray that everything gets done and that we're all wise with our time so that we're not racing around like crazy people tomorrow morning.

Prayer idea for this hour: It's tempting to rush through daily routines (especially at the end of the day), but take a minute to thank Jesus for this season of parenting, and ask for his help in soaking it in while you can. Someday you'll miss these moments, and you'll be grateful that you took the time to be thankful today.

8 P.M. TO 9 P.M.

Dear Jesus,

I pray over this coming night—that you'd help the kids get to sleep. I pray over their thoughts and worries, that they'd learn how to let things go and hand them over to you. Help them to sleep well. Protect them from sickness and bad dreams and anything else that would disturb them or harm their innocence tonight.

Prayer idea for this hour: Ask Jesus for his protection over your kids as they sleep, and over any specific worries they're struggling with as they end their day. Also ask for wisdom in protecting them from evil while still giving them a chance to grow through challenge.

9 P.M. TO 10 P.M.

Dear Jesus,

I MADE IT. Thank you for this time to relax and do grown-up things like talk to my husband and catch up with friends on social media. I pray over this time, that you'd be as present in my rest as you are in my busyness. Remind me about the things I need to prepare so that tomorrow will go smoothly (or as smoothly as possible), and help me to let go of what went undone today. And is it bad to pray for some comic relief?

Because I could use definitely use some.

Prayer idea for this hour: Ask Jesus for favor over your relationships with friends, family, coworkers, and your spouse (if you're married), and to show you any ways you can reach out to be a good friend/partner tonight. Also thank him for refilling your tank and helping you relax.

10 P.M. TO 11 P.M.

Dear Jesus,

The day went by so fast. *All* the days go by fast. Sometimes I feel like I'm just going through the motions—just trying to get through the day until evening, and then trying to get through the evening so I can sleep. And then repeat. I don't want to live my days on autopilot; I want to feel purpose, like my life means something. Please make my purpose known to me. Help me not to live tomorrow on autopilot.

Prayer idea for this hour: Ask Jesus to show you areas in which you're feeling discouraged and to give you encouragement and perspective. And ask for his ideas about how you can be more purposeful each day.

11 P.M. TO MIDNIGHT

Dear Jesus,

Okay, so it's going to be one of *those* nights. I'm lying here in bed, and I can't get to sleep because my thoughts are racing around like yippy, hyper dogs. Jesus, please bring peace to my frazzled mind. Silence my thoughts. I feel like I'm always praying for help in surrendering my worries to you (which gets old), but I'm just going to keep asking anyway because obviously I haven't nailed surrender yet. Thanks for your patience and grace.

Prayer idea for this hour: Ask Jesus to calm your thoughts and help you sleep. If you need to, surrender your worries one by one by acknowledging what you're anxious about and then saying, "Jesus, I lay this worry at your feet. Please take it from me."

MIDNIGHT TO 1 A.M.

Dear Jesus,

Blast! Just when I'd finally fallen asleep, I was awakened. I don't think I've had a full night's sleep since I became a mom. And now my mind is racing again. Please, I'd trade diamonds and beach vacations right now for the ability to fall asleep again FAST. I release my worries to you. *Again.* I surrender my to-do list and my concerns.

Again. Thank you for your peace—that you send it to me when I ask. Please keep my family safe. Amen.

Prayer idea for this hour: Ask Jesus to protect your slumber and for his mercy when your sleep is interrupted. Thank him for restoring you through sleep, and trust that he's caring for your whole, tired self.

1 A.M. TO 2 A.M.

Zzzzzz.

Prayer idea for this hour: As in the previous hour, continue to reach out to Jesus anytime your sleep is interrupted. Ask him to resolve the interruption and to supernaturally restore your body, regardless of the amount of sleep you're getting.

2 A.M. TO 3 A.M.

Dear Jesus,

The middle of the night seems so long and dark. Since I'm already awake (again), I pray for people who are awake right now, too. Maybe some of them are sick and in pain, or scared and worried. Please send your Spirit to help them. Comfort the weary, and protect the vulnerable. Please ease their suffering and get them safely through the night to a new day. Bring the dawn quickly. (Except maybe for me. Could you delay it just a little so I can sleep some more?)

Prayer idea for this hour: The middle of the night is a good time to pray for others who might be suffering, including friends, family, and people around the world. Ask Jesus to put people on your mind to pray for. Send your prayers to help them get through the night.

3 A.M. TO 4 A.M.

Zzzzzz.

Prayer idea for this hour: As in the previous hour, if you're awakened during this time, consider the possibility that Jesus might be rousing you to pray for others who are having a difficult night. Ask him to give them peaceful dreams, comfort, relief, and rest.

4 A.M. TO 5 A.M.

Dear Jesus,

Noooooo. Not. Quite. Yet. I'm not ready for it to be morning yet. I'm too warm and comfy to get up. Stretch out these last few moments of sleep and do some kind of crazy Jesus-thing where you multiply the good effects of the little sleep I got. You know—like the loaves and fishes, only with sleep. You can do that, right? I don't want to think about everything ahead of me today, so I'm going to just roll over and sleep some more and hope it lasts *forever*.

Prayer idea for this hour: Ask Jesus to help you resist the temptation to prematurely pick up the coming day's worries, concerns, and to-do list.

5 A.M. TO 6 A.M.

Dear Jesus,

I can see the light ever so slightly peeking through the windows. It's almost dawn, and my day starts soon. In this micro-moment of quiet before I really have to get serious and get up, my heart is full of gratitude. Thank you for this day. I know I whine and complain a lot, but you have given me so much. Help me to start this new day with love and patience and joy.

Prayer idea for this hour: Thank Jesus for a new day, and ask for his strength, wisdom, and guidance. Most of all, ask for his joy and purpose to fill your heart before your feet even touch the ground.

Your Day-in-a-Mom's-Life Prayer Worksheet

You know your schedule best, so here's a special prayer-planning worksheet for you. Spend five minutes thinking about your most important hours (or the hours you know tend to give you the most trouble), and write down ideas for the prayers you know you'll need most. Then keep turning back to them throughout the year.

_____

_____

_____

_____

_____

_____

_____

_____

_____

_____

_____

_____

week twenty-five

When feeling exposed is a good thing

Exposure is an early lesson in motherhood. Whether it's the immodesty of giving birth or the invasiveness of the adoption process, you and all your stuff are laid out for others to see.

This exposure just continues as kids get older. When they're young, for instance, *they say things*. Things that should remain private. Things that are secret. They say them in the grocery aisle or at the park—loudly, for all to hear. Then they get older and more sophisticated and articulate, and they begin to point out things about your shortcomings, weaknesses, and failures.

It's like being on the delivery table or in the adoption interview all over again—you're exposed for others to see.

This exposure is intimate and makes you feel vulnerable, which is uncomfortable. But know that in the midst of it, Jesus is the guardian of your heart. He values exposure because it reveals truth, but he will not exploit your vulnerability, nor will he let others exploit it. Like a photographer developing film, Jesus knows exactly how much exposure will bring out the very best image. Trust him to develop you in his way, even if it makes you uncomfortable.

For more, read Philippians 4:7.

"Then you will experience God's peace,

which exceeds anything we can understand.

His peace will guard your hearts and minds

as you live in Christ Jesus" (PHILIPPIANS 4:7).

THE JESUS INTERRUPTION
Pay Attention to Physical Cues

Think about the decisions you're facing this week. As you ponder each one, pay attention to how your chest or stomach reacts. Do you tense up? Do you expand and relax? Isolate all the decisions that are causing you to feel physically tense, and, one by one, take them to Jesus. Ask for direction, and then wait on his peace.

How Has Jesus Interrupted You Lately?

Writing things down helps us see how much we're growing, so spend 60 seconds listing every connection, interruption, insight, and word that you've shared with Jesus recently.

_____

_____

_____

_____

_____

_____

_____

_____

_____

_____

_____

_____

_____

week twenty-six

Don't overlook misfit gifts.

You don't need someone else to tell you that your child has gifts. You see them clearly every day. (Well, maybe not every day. We all have our off days.) You see the wonderful things God has placed in his heart, specifically crafted to enable him to reach the world with Jesus' love.

But there are schemes afoot designed to squelch these gifts. Some schemes are overt obstacles, like illness or failure. Others are more subtle, like being distracted by what's cool and popular.

And then there's the temptation to cater to the gifts and talents the world values. Like intelligence and athleticism and the ability to win over friends. Sometimes your child's gifts align with these values, but other times they don't. It's tempting to ignore the ones that don't fit as well, somehow thinking the contributions of the kid who likes to serve behind the scenes even when no one notices are less important than those of the kid who excels publicly in sports or on stage. Jesus often uses these less noticeable gifts to humble the proud and spread his love.

Ask Jesus to show you any gifts that you're overlooking because they don't fit, then for ideas about how to nurture them, too. Trust that he's molding your child into his masterpiece.

For more, read 1 Peter 4:10 and 1 Corinthians 12:4.

> *"God has given each of you a gift from his great variety of spiritual gifts. Use them well to serve one another"* (1 PETER 4:10).

THE JESUS INTERRUPTION
Affirm Your Child's Gifts

In three minutes or less, make a list of gifts and talents you see in your child. Then make a point to share your list with your child this week. Repeat with other family members. Bonus points for including friends.

_____

_____

_____

_____

_____

_____

_____

week
twenty-seven

**When being a mom feels terrifying,
remember this.**

You expected challenges when you learned you'd be a mom. You knew it would stretch you and test you and expose your weaknesses. But what you didn't expect was how *terrifying* being a mom is. Now your heart is exposed to the possibility of heartbreak you can't fathom.

What if your child gets sick? Like *really* sick? What if he gets lured into addiction? What if he rebels and breaks off his relationship with you, cutting you out of his life? What if he forsakes his faith? What if he dies prematurely, leaving you to deal with the black hole left by his absence?

None of these things is tolerable; each one feels like it could be your undoing.

If only you could have reassurance that none of these things will happen. But you know that's not possible, so instead you try to keep out as much danger as you can. It's exhausting, but it helps you sleep at night. *Sometimes*.

Incidentally, Jesus does have a remedy for the things that scare us in the night. His solution to overcoming terror is love. Specifically, his love. This is not a love that guarantees a smooth road, but it is a love that's sufficient for each new day—even the scary ones. Receive his love today, and let it fill your mother's heart with courage.

For more, read 1 John 4:18.

"Such love has no fear, because perfect love expels all fear" (1 JOHN 4:18).

THE JESUS INTERRUPTION
Destroy Fear
On a separate piece of paper, write down the things you're most afraid of. Now destroy your list. Crumple it, and pitch it in the trash. Compost it. Burn it to a crisp. Do this as a symbol of letting go of fear as you receive Jesus' comfort and courage.

week twenty-eight

Jesus' surprising offer for your failure

You arrived late to morning drop-off. *Again*. And when you got home and spotted the lunch bag on the counter, you realized why you'd been feeling a nagging sensation that you'd left something behind.

You lost your temper two times before lunch. Your errands took three times as long as you'd planned. And you only made it through half of your to-do list. And that was actually a *good* day.

Perpetually falling short is something you'll never get used to as a mom. The humbling sense of failure follows you like a shadow. And because it makes you feel ashamed, you combat failure by trying to have or be enough. Enough patience for the witching hour. Enough nutritional food on the table. Enough attention for each kid. Enough affection left over for your spouse. Some days you get close to your goal and feel it's actually possible to defeat failure. Other days...well, ice cream pick-me-ups become your consolation prize.

Hear this: Failure may make you feel ashamed, but Jesus is not ashamed of your failure. It's not even his plan to remove failure from your life because failure makes you more inclined to depend on him, which is his desire for you. A perfectly put-together mom with no needs is a mom who doesn't need him, either. He wants your closeness more than your success and is offering to take away your shame in the bargain. Make the deal; embrace your shortcomings. You won't come up short.

For more, read 2 Corinthians 12:9-10.

"*Each time he said, 'My grace is all you need. My power works best in weakness.' So now I am glad to boast about my weaknesses, so that the power of Christ can work through me. That's why I take pleasure in my weaknesses, and in the insults, hardships, persecutions, and troubles that I suffer for Christ. For when I am weak, then I am strong*" (2 CORINTHIANS 12:9-10).

THE JESUS INTERRUPTION
Recognize Your Limitations

This is your "quiet time" this week: Once a day, where other people aren't watching (or in public, if you're confident like that), do a set of pushups until your arms feel like they're going to give out. Then remind yourself that your own strength has very defined limitations and that Jesus is strong in your weaknesses, not your strengths. Think about one area where you're relying on your own strength, and hand it over to Jesus.

week
twenty-nine

**Kids' greatest freedom is
from themselves.**

Oh, no, she's spotted her. You were hoping your daughter wouldn't notice the sweet little girl setting up a dinner of fake food for her plastic family. But now your daughter sees her.

In a flash your daughter is at her side, aggressively grabbing for the toy. "Mine," she says. The wailing starts, and the tug-of-war intensifies.

So it begins. The *selfishness*. We're all born with it, and your wonderful, gifted, unique child is no different. Snatching someone's toys is eventually replaced by more sophisticated expressions of self-interest, like sibling rivalry, a fixed obsession with getting what she wants, and a complete inability to see another person's perspective (I'm talking to you, teenagers of the world).

This selfishness is both frustrating and understandable. You recognize it in yourself; as a mom you've learned to put others' needs before your own, but you've had your share of wailing, too. Ultimately the thing that helped you is the same thing that can help your child: the Holy Spirit directing her focus off herself and onto Jesus. Perhaps the greatest freedom Jesus offers is to set us free from ourselves, and he will help your child discover this freedom.

For more, read Romans 6:7.

> *"For when we died with Christ we were set free from the power of sin"* (ROMANS 6:7).

THE JESUS INTERRUPTION

Focus on a New Name

This week ask Jesus to give you a creative adjective or name for each member of your family that incorporates a special, unique truth about each one. Then use this adjective every time you pray for them, and think about creative ways you can affirm this truth in their lives this week.

week thirty

Help for your wish list

If you could make a mom's wish list, I'm betting that it would include the following:

A prayer to be more certain of your decisions instead of always second-guessing yourself or comparing yourself to other moms.

A desire to be stable: more organized, disciplined, and consistent.

And a hope for steadiness—to leave emotional roller coasters in the past.

This is an admirable list. Each and every one of these things is possible...only not for you. (Gosh, that sounds harsh. Please keep reading.) This list is not possible for you in your own strength. Even on your strongest, best, most resolute days, you're still weak. You'll always be susceptible to indecision and comparison, to insecurity and I-couldn't-be-rational-right-now-if-you-paid-me emotionalism.

But hear Jesus when he says this, because it's different from what you'll hear elsewhere: Your weakness is *welcome*. Jesus isn't turned off by it; he doesn't need you to try harder to be stronger. In fact, he'd prefer to be the strong one. So why not let him? Today embrace your weakness and lean on his strength. He's strong enough to make your wish list possible.

For more, read 1 Corinthians 1:27.

> *"God chose things the world considers foolish in order to shame those who think they are wise. And he chose things that are powerless to shame those who are powerful"*
>
> (1 CORINTHIANS 1:27).

THE JESUS INTERRUPTION
Dismiss Sneaky Lies Disguised as Motivational Messages

This week pay attention to any headlines that talk about how you can and deserve to have it all. Each time you read, see, or hear this message, actively dismiss it by scoffing, saying "whatever," or using the phrase "That's poppycock." (For the record, I recommend this last option.) Each time, remember that you already have it all with Jesus.

How Has Jesus Interrupted You Lately?

Writing things down helps us see how much we're growing, so spend 60 seconds listing every connection, interruption, insight, and word that you've shared with Jesus recently.

_____

_____

_____

_____

_____

_____

_____

_____

_____

_____

_____

_____

_____

week
thirty-one

Permission to be childlike?
Granted.

Anything can be a toy. Sticks. Cotton balls. Bugs.

Any afternoon is perfect for daydreaming.

Any goal is possible.

There's nothing like being around kids to remind yourself that you aren't one anymore. You envy their imagination and their rejection of limitations. You wish for their playfulness and disregard for worries and responsibilities.

But their freedom comes at a price, right? Childhood is only possible because adults protect it with their willingness to take on responsibility. It's a bargain you gladly make, a gift you gladly give.

What if I told you it's possible to protect your child's freedom while also reclaiming some of it for yourself? Because you can.

Jesus would like to remind you that you've been offered the same gift of freedom that your child has. As a child of God, you're set free from the burdens of worry. You're free to create. Free to give openly. Free to trust. Free to play.

This idea is difficult to embrace because carefree can look like carelessness from the outside, and being "childish" is frowned upon. But those frowns and judgments aren't coming from God. He wants for you what you want for your child: to preserve the sacredness of your heart, and to cherish it fondly. And he's taken responsibility for your worries and cares. So go ahead—be God's child and go out and play.

For more, read Matthew 6:28-33.

"Seek the Kingdom of God above all else, and live righteously, and he will give you everything you need" (MATTHEW 6:33).

THE JESUS INTERRUPTION
Reclaim the Freedom of Childhood

Practice being a kid this week. Color. Craft. Run outside. Be silly. Whatever makes you feel carefree, do it as many times as you can this week.

week thirty-two

Take heart—there's peace for your anxious child.

She's doing it again—biting her nails. She always does that when she's anxious. Judging by her nearly bleeding nailbeds, the anxiety has been constant lately.

There are few things more difficult than watching your child in distress. You hate to see her anxious or afraid, especially if that anxiety is keeping her from doing things she'd enjoy. You desperately want her to have a *childhood*, not to spend her youth fretting about problems the way adults do.

While it's tempting to let her anxiety make *you* anxious, here's the thing to focus on: Jesus offers your child peace and freedom from anxiety. This doesn't always look like instant relief; sometimes it comes in minute-by-minute doses, requiring patience and faith. Hang in there, and believe that Jesus is working to help your child overcome anxiety and rely on his strength.

For more, read 1 Peter 5:7.

"Give all your worries and cares to God, for he cares about you" (1 PETER 5:7).

THE JESUS INTERRUPTION

Picture Anxiety's Defeat

The next time your child battles anxiety, try this visual exercise: Picture her surrounded by bullies seeking to intimidate her. Then picture Jesus approaching the crowd. Watch what he does to the bullies and the impact it has on your child. Then thank Jesus for his protection against things that are bullying your child into anxiety. Repeat this every time the anxiety returns.

week thirty-three

Your forgetfulness doesn't annoy Jesus.

I have a prediction about you. I predict that sometime within the next 48 hours you'll start a sentence with, "How many times do I have to tell you to...?"

I also predict that your voice will *not* be calm and measured when you say this.

It's true that one of the more frustrating aspects of being a mom is the constant nagging. You really don't want to nag; in fact, you'd much prefer not to. But *seriously*—without 1,000 daily reminders about everything from picking up shoes to doing homework, *nothing* would get done. Even with nagging, you still end up at Hobby Lobby five minutes before closing time, searching for felt and paint for the project you just found out about—that's due tomorrow.

In other words, your kids have memories like that fish in *Finding Nemo*. (And because you're a mom, you know exactly what fish I'm talking about.)

Turns out, you have a bad memory, too. When it comes to Jesus' words, you're nearly as forgetful as your kids are. You start your morning, for instance, determined not to worry about tomorrow (per Jesus' advice) and then promptly spend the entire day fixated on future problems.

And so, like your kids, you need many, *many* reminders. Fortunately, this doesn't annoy Jesus. He repeated important truths frequently during his time on Earth, and he's been repeating them ever since. He'll do the same for you—1,000 times a day if you need it.

For more, read Romans 2:4.

"*Don't you see how wonderfully kind, tolerant, and patient God is with you? Does this mean nothing to you? Can't you see that his kindness is intended to turn you from your sin?*" (ROMANS 2:4).

THE JESUS INTERRUPTION
Be a Nag

Every time you find yourself nagging a child this week, immediately ask Jesus to remind you about a lesson you're forgetting. Then invite him to put the lesson in front of you in obvious ways all day.

week
thirty-four

Stop babysitting the clock.

As Mom, you're the Ultimate Timekeeper. Your word establishes bedtime. You decide when to leave in the morning, and when curfew is. You're the timer of chores, screen time, and the Silent Game while Mommy is driving. For all intents and purposes, your watch runs the show.

You know the truth, though, which is that you do not control time. Not. Even. A. Little. If you did, the things you're currently waiting on would be HERE ALREADY. You know what I'm talking about—those prayer requests that are taking FOREVER to be answered. The ones making you antsy and maybe even a little angry.

Jesus talked a lot about timing during his earthly life. And the right timing was always set by God's watch, not his. Even now he's waiting on God's timing—waiting to return and claim his inheritance as King. (You think you've been waiting a long time! Try 2,000 years and counting.)

So *calm down already* and receive the aid of one of those fruits of the Spirit: patience. God's timing is always moving faster and slower than we think it should, but he knows what he's doing.

For more, read Colossians 1:11-12 and James 1:2-4.

"Dear brothers and sisters, when troubles of any kind come your way, consider it an opportunity for great joy. For you know that when your faith is tested, your endurance has a chance to grow. So let it grow, for when your endurance is fully developed, you will be perfect and complete, needing nothing" (JAMES 1:2-4).

THE JESUS INTERRUPTION
Go Off Plan

For a day this week, ditch your planner, routine, alarm, or timer and open yourself up to spontaneity. Invite Jesus to direct your agenda, and enjoy the excitement of not knowing what's coming next.

week thirty-five

**Go ahead—feel guilty.
Just don't stay there.**

Breaking news: Apparently moms struggle with feeling guilty. Like *all the time.* Guilty for not spending more time with their kids. Guilty for losing patience and yelling. Guilty for saying no and saying yes, guilty for not saying either.

Wait—what was that? Oh…so you've already heard about this guilt thing? I see. Apparently it's not breaking news but so universal that saying "moms feel guilty" is like saying "the sky is blue." Well, all right then. Let's move on because Jesus has something to say about all this guilt.

First, he says you're right—you *are* guilty. Every. Single. Time. The standard is high, and you fall short. Sorry. Feeling guilty is a healthy part of acknowledging the truth about your helpless state. So go ahead—feel guilty. It's good for you.

But don't—I repeat, *don't*—stay there, stuck in those feelings. Because that's where you're getting hung up. You're judging yourself, and that's not your job. Jesus is the only judge worth paying any attention to, and he has no condemnation for you. He has set you free from judgment. So the next time you feel guilty, acknowledge your helpless state, and then let Jesus take your guilt away. He died for the privilege to do so. Don't rob him of that pleasure.

For more, read Romans 8:1.

> "*So now there is no condemnation for those who belong to Christ Jesus*" (ROMANS 8:1).

THE JESUS INTERRUPTION
Draw a Symbol of Freedom
Draw a small balloon in pen on your wrist today. Every time you look at it, remember that your guilt and shortcomings float away from you because Jesus sets you free. Bonus: Imagine him popping every balloon. Seriously—it's fun.

How Has Jesus Interrupted You Lately?

Writing things down helps us see how much we're growing, so spend 60 seconds listing every connection, interruption, insight, and word that you've shared with Jesus recently.

_____

_____

_____

_____

_____

_____

_____

_____

_____

_____

_____

_____

_____

_____

week
thirty-six

On raising a rule-breaker

Imagine that starting today, your child is set free from all rules.

I'm not sure what you're picturing right now, but I'm envisioning sticky-fingered kids consuming all-ice-cream diets and teens roaming the streets until 2 a.m., unencumbered by curfews. No one would be in school ever, and the stores would run out of junk food.

Let's call it The Ice Cream Curfew Apocalypse.

Of course this would never actually happen. But one part of this scenario is true: Your child *is* free from rules. Not *your* rules, exactly (so don't let him con you into that), but free from trying to live up to the world's rules.

During Jesus' day, there were rules about when to do things, who to be friends with, and what to do with your life. Though the rules are different today, your child faces the same types of rules and pressures today. You can give him permission and encouragement to break these rules by following Jesus' example of listening to God's voice and going a new way.

For more, read Galatians 5:1.

> *"So Christ has truly set us free. Now make sure that you stay free, and don't get tied up again in slavery to the law"* (GALATIANS 5:1).

THE JESUS INTERRUPTION
Break the Rules
With your child, pick a day this week to have breakfast for dinner, to stay up past bedtime to do something fun, or to play hooky. Make it your "break the rules" day, and thank Jesus together each time you enjoy the liberty.

week
thirty-seven

You have a purpose, and it's not just to be a mom.

Remember when you were a little girl, rocking your doll to sleep, feeding her plastic food, and changing her outfits? You dreamed of becoming a mom.

Now as a mom of a real child, your dream has come true. And it's wonderful—except, of course, when it's not. It's during these not-so-dreamy times that you may find yourself asking, "Is this it? Am I living out my purpose?"

The answer is no…but yes, too.

If by "Is this it?" you're wondering if your life was meant for only mothering, then no. You have a purpose, and it's not just being a mom. Your purpose includes partnering with Jesus on his world-changing mission to make all things new. This includes your child, but extends beyond her, too. This mission incorporates your gifts, some of which have very little to do with parenting. And it embraces a lot of other people who don't call you Mom or repeatedly ask for food.

If, however, by "Is this it?" you're wondering if your purpose is perhaps less glamorous than it seemed as a starry-eyed youth, then yes, your purpose is less glamorous than you imagined. Jesus' purpose was to take up his cross, and he said ours would be the same. Taking up your cross looks a lot more like what you already do every day—serving others, caring for their needs, putting yourself last—than like the world's glittery definition of success. Don't be fooled by contemporary ideas of purpose that promise thrill and earthly reward.

True purpose is much plainer, and much, *much* more rewarding. So stay the course. You're on the right path. **For more, read Luke 9:23.**

"Then he said to the crowd, 'If any of you wants to be my follower, you must give up your own way, take up your cross daily, and follow me'" (LUKE 9:23).

THE JESUS INTERRUPTION
Reconnect With Your Pre-Mom Self

Think of one thing you used to enjoy before you became a mom, and then ask Jesus to show you one baby step you can take to reconnect to this interest this week.

week
thirty-eight

Jesus beats Pinterest every time.

According to PIN 5:3 (that stands for Pinterest, board 5, pin 3, by the way), a good mom shall gain mastery over kids' media time and Internet safety protocols. PIN 7:12 says that a good mom shall provide no less than three organic snacks per day, and avoid HFCS (high fructose corn syrup, of course) at all costs. And PIN 12:2 says that a good mom provides the perfect balance of open yet firm discipline, as evidenced by her well-behaved children.

Of course, nowhere on Pinterest does it say, "A good mom sits on her fanny with ne'er a care in the world while everyone else works hard."

Pinterest doesn't say that, but Jesus did. When two sisters were entertaining him, one was doing all the right, responsible things, and the other was lounging with Jesus. He praised the latter, and then told the former to put down her busywork already and join them. To paraphrase, "You're distracted by the wrong things," he said.

So put down your busywork—your Pinterest rules and organic snacks and perfect discipline tactics. Turn your attention to what really matters: Jesus. Let him tell you what's important, because it's definitely not what's keeping everyone else so needlessly busy. Erase what you know about what good moms do, and let him surprise you with his ideas for you instead. I think you'll find that he beats Pinterest every time.

For more, read Luke 10:38-42.

"The Lord said to her, 'My dear Martha, you are worried and upset over all these details! There is only one thing worth being concerned about. Mary has discovered it, and it will not be taken away from her'" (Luke 10:41–42).

THE JESUS INTERRUPTION
Give Yourself a Parenting Grade

Using the space provided, make a report card for your parenting by writing down every aspect of parenting you can think of (discipline, consistency, proper nutrition, affection, etc.), and then give yourself an honest grade for each. Then cross off every grade and write Jesus' name instead, remembering that your value is not measured by your parenting but by him alone.

REPORT CARD

Parenting Task	Grade

week thirty-nine

**Your boundaries are blurry.
Jesus can help with that.**

It's happened again. You casually mention to your playgroup that your 5-year-old has started acting up in preschool, and suddenly you're buried under comments and advice.

"She's probably not getting enough sleep. Have you tried melatonin? My sister swears by it for her kids."

"We've just put Michael on a gluten-free diet, and the difference has been amazing. Maybe you should try it."

"Things have been pretty tense between you and your husband lately, right? Could it be that she's watching you argue and is acting out because of it? Maybe you should be extra sensitive to what you say around her."

And so on.

Within five minutes your head is swimming. You respect all of their opinions and don't want to hurt their feelings by dismissing their ideas, but where do you start? Here's an idea: Start with Jesus. He loves how much you care about other people. He doesn't, however, love how much you care about *what other people think*.

When you place a high premium on the opinions of others, it becomes easy for them to start bossing you around. This bossing may not be overt, which makes it sneaky. Rather than telling you what to do (which happens sometimes, too), you start shaping your decisions around what you *think* they want you to do. It doesn't take very long before you're overextended, stressed, and a little resentful.

When you're feeling this way, remember that Jesus

has a unique perspective on your life and direct insight into what you can handle (it's often both more and less than what you think you can handle). It frustrates him when you say yes to things that are too much for you, and no to things that will challenge and grow you. He doesn't like to see your boundaries stretched too far in some areas (usually to accommodate someone else's expectations), and not enough in others (to accommodate your own expectations). If you ask him, he will show you what your true boundaries should be. And then he will help you maintain them.

For more, read Galatians 1:10.

"Obviously, I'm not trying to win the approval of people, but of God. If pleasing people were my goal, I would not be Christ's servant" (GALATIANS 1:10).

THE JESUS INTERRUPTION
Set a Tight Boundary

Using the space provided, write all the things that are
stressing you out today. Then ask Jesus to help you
visualize and draw boundary lines around each one.
Notice which things have tight boundaries around
them, and which boundaries are looser and wider.
(Some of these might surprise you.) Focus on the tight
boundaries, and pray for wisdom about one way to hold
firm to one of them today.

_____

_____

_____

_____

_____

_____

_____

_____

_____

week forty

When you're out of ideas...

There are moments—so many moments—in parenting when you're just out of ideas.

Your toddler has vehemently resisted every attempt to help her overcome her separation anxiety, leaving you exhausted and bewildered in the wake of her red-hot rage.

Your preteen has flippantly brushed off every effort to get him to open up about the teasing he's experiencing at school. You know it's happening, but he dodges every question, leaving you frustrated and worried.

These are the situations that cause you to feel bankrupt as a parent. If you can't troubleshoot these problems—some trivial, some serious—who will? It's up to you, and your toolbox is empty.

But here's the thing. Jesus is *not* out of tools. His toolbox is full of unexpected, creative, and persuasive tools, each sharpened and ready for the specific fix you need. So ask him, "What now?" and wait for him to respond. He promises that he will shower you with kindness, wisdom, and understanding when you're out of ideas.

For more, read Ephesians 1:3.

"All praise to God, the Father of our Lord Jesus Christ, who has blessed us with every spiritual blessing in the heavenly realms because we are united with Christ"
(EPHESIANS 1:3).

THE JESUS INTERRUPTION
Give Abundant, Undivided Attention
The next time you're feeling stuck as a parent and out of ideas, try slowing down and paying really close attention to your child. As you carefully listen to his words and watch his expressions and body language, ask Jesus to open your eyes to things you've been missing, and to see your child's heart beneath the surface.

How Has Jesus Interrupted You Lately?

Writing things down helps us see how much we're growing, so spend 60 seconds listing every connection, interruption, insight, and word that you've shared with Jesus recently.

_____

_____

_____

_____

_____

_____

_____

_____

_____

_____

_____

_____

_____

week
forty-one

On sharing custody

She has your eyes. And that quirky thing you do with your food? She does it, too.

He's sensitive just as you were at his age; only he tries to hide it. But you know his heart, because it's your heart, too.

We are imprinted on our kids. Their biology, behaviors, and quirky mannerisms remind us of our own. Whether they came from our womb or were adopted into our lives, our kids are most definitely *our kids*.

Which is why it's easy for you to forget one important truth: Your child is God's child, too. God is the original parent, and you're in partnership with him. This partnership is both a relief and unnerving.

A relief because you're not alone—you have a powerful parenting ally. God knows things about your child that you don't know. Plus, he loves your child even more than you do, which is hard to believe but true.

Here's the unnerving part: God is willing to take bigger risks with your child than you are. His safety net is broader than your comfort zone. Sometimes *a lot* broader. This riskiness can make him seem untrustworthy, but the truth is, he's better at parenting than you are. Ask for help trusting, and watch his plans unfold for the child both of you love.

For more, read 1 John 3:1.

"See how very much our Father loves us, for he calls us his children, and that is what we are!" (1 JOHN 3:1).

THE JESUS INTERRUPTION
Find the Best Gift
The next time you want to buy a gift for your child, pause before entering the store or website. Ask Jesus to lead you to the perfect gift: one that will delight and encourage your child—and challenge her to grow.

week
forty-two

Jesus has strange ideas about getting it together.

You expected fatigue during the first few years of being a mom. The nightly feedings. The restless toddlers. The long nights battling sickness. They were right: It was all as hard as they said it would be. But eventually sleep became more regular, and you started to feel sort of normal again.

Except that this new normal is still kind of exhausting, right?

Sure, there's more sleep (though not like before—never like before). But now other things tire you out. Like endless, nagging worries about your kids. And money stuff and work stuff and house stuff and marriage stuff. Which would maybe all be manageable if you had half a second to actually manage it.

In these situations (aka being a mom), you get the idea that relying on Jesus' strength means you're able to get everything under control, at least for today. But more often his strength means letting go of control—stopping your efforts to manage your weariness and worries. Because Jesus is offering to manage them *for* you. Accepting this deal means that he gets to manage things as he sees fit (ahem, which is sometimes different from your ideas), but it also means that you get peace and rest. Both ways, you win.

For more, read Matthew 11:28.

> *"Then Jesus said, 'Come to me, all of you who are weary and carry heavy burdens, and I will give you rest'"* (MATTHEW 11:28).

THE JESUS INTERRUPTION

Start Simplifying

Review your daily routine, and ask Jesus to give you three ideas for streamlining and simplifying how you're doing things. Beginning today, show Jesus which steps you can remove and which things you can stop doing altogether.

week
forty-three

You're healthy, vibrant, and growing
(not saggy, pale, and dried up).

You stand in front of the mirror, trying on yet another pair of jeans. Though it wouldn't seem that such a thing is possible, this pair is both too tight *and* too saggy.

Awesome.

You step closer, hoping to improve the angle. This is a mistake because now you can see your face under the hot dressing-room lights. It's pale, and sometime between 9 a.m. and lunch you've managed to lose all evidence of your makeup. You now look like how you feel, which is to say, old and tired.

Even more awesome.

"Is this the price of being a mom?" you wonder. A bargain whereby you trade your youth for your kid? Will you ever feel fresh and vibrant again?

The answer, dear mom, is both yes and no.

Yes, you'll feel fresh and vibrant. In fact, you can feel that today, right now. Jesus talks about being a green, fleshy, healthy vine, of which you're a branch. All the potency of his growth is yours for the taking. You need only to hold on to him.

However, if you're searching for vibrancy in youth and beauty, then no—you won't feel fresh. Every time you compare yourself with how you used to be, or to how someone else looks, you'll dry up just a little more. Because you're not holding on to Jesus—you're holding on to a different vine. A temporary vine. A vine destined to wither away.

So choose who you're going to graft on to, and choose

well. Only one vine can offer you true life (and less frustration in the dressing room).

For more, read John 15:1-5.

"Yes, I am the vine; you are the branches. Those who remain in me, and I in them, will produce much fruit. For apart from me you can do nothing" (JOHN 15:5).

THE JESUS INTERRUPTION
See Your True Identity in the Mirror

The next time you're in front of the mirror, pause 60 seconds and ask Jesus to give you one word he uses to describe you. What do you hear? (Note: If this word makes you feel shame, you're letting your inner mean girl talk over Jesus. Ask him to speak up, and keep listening until the shame is gone.)

week
forty-four

The thing that matters most is actually
not something you can achieve.

"If, at the end of the day, your child is saved, then you've done your job as a parent."

If you're nodding your head in agreement with this quote, you're not alone. At the end of the day, it's salvation that matters, right? *Right*.

But mom—mostly this statement is a lie. It sounds really nice, but it's not true.

If your child loves Jesus, it's *exclusively* the work of the Holy Spirit, not successful parenting on your part. You can influence your child. You can set an example of love, grace, and discipleship. You can speak, teach, and model truth. But you can't save.

This can be frustrating because you're hardwired to save your child. If he fell through ice, got sick, or started failing, you'd save him. You'd find doctors and tutors and heroes—whatever it took. But when it comes to saving him from sin, you're out of your league.

Of course you know this, but it doesn't stop you from intervening if he seems off track—trying to broker his relationship with Jesus or make him see the truth, praying harder, preaching harder. But as much as you'd like to ensure your child's salvation, it's not within your power, and it's not your responsibility.

But it is *Someone's* responsibility, and he takes this work very seriously. Jesus is accountable for each and every sheep in his flock, and he attends to every one of them. So every time you feel anxious about your child's salvation, remember that Jesus is the one doing that work. Relieve yourself of that burden.

For more, read John 14:6 and John 10:1-18.

"Jesus told him, 'I am the way, the truth, and the life. No one can come to the Father except through me'" (JOHN 14:6).

THE JESUS INTERRUPTION
Show, Don't Tell

Instead of trying to *teach* your child about Jesus and how to follow him, *show* him how it looks through your own actions this week. Pray that Jesus will lead you to the behaviors that will leave the greatest impression on you and your child.

week
forty-five

**You're not what you do
(even when what you do is awesome).**

There she is again with another status update, complete with a magazine-worthy photo. This time she's made homemade bread from scratch, and yes, it looks delicious. Yesterday she announced that she'd just sent in her final car payment. And six days ago she completed her first half-marathon.

Seriously—who are these people who seem to have it all together? They're setting and accomplishing *real* goals while the rest of us are just happy to have successfully matched each sock with its partner in yesterday's laundry.

I think you know the kind of people I'm talking about. They'd be easier to dislike if we didn't envy their accomplishments so much. Or maybe you *are* this kind of person—the on-the-ball, moving-forward-with-life kind of person.

Regardless, this idea that there's a spectrum of worthy people—with bread-baking, marathon-running whizzes on one end and disheveled, mismatched-sock-wearers on the other—is *completely false*. There's no spectrum. We've fabricated it.

Here's the truth, and this is an important one: You aren't what you do. Matching socks, financial solvency, fitness—none of it adds one ounce of value in Jesus' eyes. All that matters is *his* value, *his* accomplishments. So stop the comparisons. Stop measuring your quality by the checkmarks on your to-do list. Turn your eyes to Jesus, and let him tell you what's important.

For more, read Romans 6:20-21 and Colossians 3:11.

"Christ is all that matters, and he lives in all of us" (COLOSSIANS 3:11).

THE JESUS INTERRUPTION
Leave Things Undone
As a reminder that having it all together is *not* Jesus' goal for you, decide not to clean up a few messes this week, and intentionally leave a few tasks undone.

How Has Jesus Interrupted You Lately?

Writing things down helps us see how much we're growing, so spend 60 seconds listing every connection, interruption, insight, and word that you've shared with Jesus recently.

_____

_____

_____

_____

_____

_____

_____

_____

_____

_____

_____

_____

_____

week
forty-six

**You crush darkness,
you mama warrior, you.**

You probably don't feel it in your day-to-day life. You're busy running errands, managing logistics, getting things done. In fact, you might be tempted to dismiss it altogether. But here's the truth: You're a force to be reckoned with. A dangerous force. A deadly force.

You didn't earn this power, and definitely motherhood didn't grant it to you (in spite of what the culture may say). Rather, Jesus died and defeated death and then passed this power along to you as his follower. And now, in his name you can crush darkness. This darkness looks like sin, anxiety, insecurity, sickness, bitterness, and the rest of their ilk. And it threatens to steal, kill, and destroy you and those you love.

But you're not afraid, because Jesus is by your side. He said you'll crush the head of the devil, so start stomping.

For more, read 1 Corinthians 15:57.

"But thank God! He gives us victory over sin and death through our Lord Jesus Christ" (1 CORINTHIANS 15:57).

THE JESUS INTERRUPTION
Wage a Little Warfare

Practice no-frills spiritual warfare this week by calling out negativity and yuckiness by name. For example, say "Critical spirit, we don't need you here today. Jesus, please escort it out" or "Jesus, I see doubt has decided to join us. Please remove it. Thanks."

week forty-seven

Stop hiding your good parts.

You're not sure why some things are so easy for you. You've heard friends and other moms talk about how difficult those same things are for them, and you nod your head as if to agree, not wanting to stand out as the oddball.

Why do you do that? Why do you intentionally work to level the playing field, playing up hard and challenging things? Jesus has given you strengths as a woman and a mom. He did not mean for you to chuck them out, choosing to focus instead on your weaknesses to make everyone around you feel comfortable.

Dear mom—it's okay to acknowledge and enjoy your gifts. It's okay to recognize what you're naturally good at, and to (Gasp!) talk about those gifts with others. Not to brag. But to genuinely enjoy and share with an open, generous heart. That's what gifts are for: to use—and to re-gift.

And yes, it's okay to acknowledge your weaknesses, too. Jesus embraces your weaknesses and uses them as a way to show his strength. But that's different from your showcasing them because you feel it's the proper, humble, or modest thing to do. That's just the other side of the bragging coin. So toss that coin and invest the one you've been given. I believe Jesus calls that one your *talent*.

For more, read Ephesians 2:10.

"For we are God's masterpiece. He has created us anew in Christ Jesus, so we can do the good things he planned for us long ago" (EPHESIANS 2:10).

THE JESUS INTERRUPTION
Notice What Comes Naturally

Think about three things that are coming naturally to you right now and write them in the space provided. They can relate to being a mom or to something else. Now every time this week you're tempted to downplay these strengths or dwell on failure, mentally revisit your list and take confidence in the truth that you have gifts and are using them.

_____

_____

_____

_____

week forty-eight

The thing your kid doesn't deserve

No one ever tells you how your kids will break your heart as a mom. If you're nodding your head in agreement, thinking about all the times your heart breaks with compassion when you see your child hurting or sad, I don't think you get my point.

I'm talking about the times your kid breaks your heart by hurting *your* feelings and making *you* sad. Those are some of the worst times as a mom.

To make matters worse, you aren't the only one your kids will hurt. Eventually they'll hurt others and fall from grace and act selfishly and sin. A lot. (Even the good kids.)

For these times, your child needs something that she doesn't deserve: forgiveness. Fortunately, forgiveness is in Jesus' nature. It is his special work, and he's very good at it. He won't hold your child's shortcomings against her. He washes the slate clean every time, giving your child a fresh allotment of grace and forgiveness and the potential to heal rather than hurt. So when you're feeling heartbroken, heave a deep sigh of relief as you thank Jesus for his all-encompassing forgiveness.

For more, read Ephesians 4:32 and 1 John 2:12.

"Instead, be kind to each other, tenderhearted, forgiving one another, just as God through Christ has forgiven you"

(EPHESIANS 4:32).

THE JESUS INTERRUPTION
Erase Hurt

Ask Jesus to bring to mind hurts and disappointments that you're still carrying around with you. Then open a note on your smartphone and list each one. Finally, erase each hurt, one by one, as you pray for Jesus' help to forgive the guilty parties, even if they've never asked for your forgiveness.

J.

week
forty-nine

That thing you know but keep forgetting

THE JESUS
INTERRUPTION

I'm about to say that thing you know is true but still need lots of reminders of. Here it is: You're not defined by the success or failure of your kids.

Yes, yes, nod, nod. Of course you agree. Jesus died on the cross, and you are defined by him, right? Except it's not so easy to believe that when your kid is struggling in school and pulling low grades. Or when he's doing really well in sports and you're all puffed up like a proud mother hen. Or when he's being mean and other people are watching.

When these things happen, you're worried, elated, ashamed...(fill in the emotion, depending on the failure or victory at hand). Your kid feels like your very heart, walking around outside your body. When he falters, you falter. When he triumphs, you triumph. And if he's doing bad things, you're bad.

Except this isn't true. You're measured by precisely one thing and one thing only: Jesus. Your kid may feel like your heart, but Jesus is the spirit inside you. There are no grades with Jesus—not even parenting ones. There is no success and no failure, except the victory of his salvation. I don't care how many times you need to hear it—maybe every day for the next 20 years. It doesn't matter. Whatever it takes to remind you that you're defined by Jesus, and his judgment over you is pure love. So keep nodding your head in agreement. Eventually it'll sink in.

For more, read John 14:27.

"I am leaving you with a gift—peace of mind and heart. And the peace I give is a gift the world cannot give. So don't be troubled or afraid" (JOHN 14:27).

THE JESUS INTERRUPTION
Find Free Time

Look at your calendar this week and ask Jesus to help you spot any open spaces—even short ones. Pencil in time to connect with him in those slots. Use it to study, pray, or read a devotion if you want, but it's okay to just relax, too. He'll gladly join you either way.

week fifty

**When you feel like you're stuck
in a rut, remember this.**

Brain science is all the rage today. (Well, maybe not the rage. It's exciting for moderately science-y moms who like to geek out over neurons.) You've maybe read a little about it because it's hard to miss all the talk about neuroplasticity and learning development and how your kid is a sponge. (No, not your kid *ate* a sponge, though that happens, too.)

Perhaps you're aware, then, that the brain adapts to patterns by creating channels. Like a river carving its way through canyon walls, it's believed that our behaviors carve pathways in our brains. This is awesome for making certain things more efficient, like, say, driving to the store on autopilot and changing diapers without even thinking about it. It's less awesome, however, when it keeps us stuck in bad patterns.

These bad patterns are usually rooted in our sinful nature. You know—that stubborn, selfish will inside of you that does what you don't want it to do. As a mom or spouse or friend or coworker, these patterns often cause you to let yourself and others down.

That's the bad news. Here's the good news: Jesus is doing a new thing in you. He's replaced your sinful self with his Spirit. This means that he's already begun to carve new channels—*his* channels. The more you spend time in his presence, the deeper those channels get. They make his thoughts and his behaviors and his feelings more efficient inside you, so that they become your nature, too.

Pretty soon he'll rewire your old ways with his new ways.

For more, read 2 Corinthians 5:17.

"This means that anyone who belongs to Christ has become a new person. The old life is gone; a new life has begun!"

(2 CORINTHIANS 5:17).

THE JESUS INTERRUPTION
Declutter Your Influencers
Give Jesus a chance to weigh in on who's influencing you by auditing the websites and social profiles you follow. Evaluate each one, asking Jesus whether he wants you to keep it or pass on it. Then, the next time you want to add a new website or profile, ask the same question.

How Has Jesus Interrupted You Lately?

Writing things down helps us see how much we're growing, so spend 60 seconds listing every connection, interruption, insight, and word that you've shared with Jesus recently.

_____

_____

_____

_____

_____

_____

_____

_____

_____

_____

_____

_____

_____

week
fifty-one

You aren't the only one who's ferociously protective.

She did it again. She tripped and fell and just avoided lacerating her head on a sharp corner. She *barely* eeked by. She missed an accident because she was stalled by a train. She was slighted by that sketchy kid she had a crush on (#praisejesus).

Yet even though she escaped, each brush with danger reminds you how dangerous the world is. Every day you ask God to protect her. Because you're the mama bear, instinctively and ferociously protective.

This protective nature comes from God, which means that you aren't carrying your ferociousness alone. His protection also surrounds your child, keeping her from harm in ways you'll never imagine (and frankly wouldn't want to). He's watching over her steps, and his Spirit is guiding her, telling her which paths to take and which ones to avoid. He's the small voice whispering to her and tugging on her gut when something is off. Letting God protect your child is hard because he's more willing to expose her to danger than you are. But he's asking you to believe that he's protecting her, and you can trust in him.

For more, read 2 Thessalonians 3:3.

> *"But the Lord is faithful; he will strengthen you and guard you from the evil one"*
>
> (2 THESSALONIANS 3:3).

THE JESUS INTERRUPTION
Midnight Prayers

When you're up in the middle of the night, instead of getting anxious, use your interrupted sleep as an opportunity to say prayers for people who are sick, lonely, and hurting, both in your life and throughout the world. The night can feel like a long, dark stretch, but you can help bring light to someone's midnight hour.

week
fifty-two

You are chosen.

It's kind of unbelievable, isn't it? This privilege of being the mother of this incredible person. In spite of the difficulties, sacrifice, and challenges, at the end of the day, you're still amazed that you were chosen for this job.

That's the thing about being chosen. You didn't *earn* your child. You were picked. It doesn't always seem fair, being a recipient of this favor. For instance, you know people who can't have kids. You know people who've lost children. You don't deserve the honor any more than they do, and yet you have it anyway.

It's the same way with Jesus. He chose you to be part of his family. Not because you earned it or deserve it, but because it's his favor. It's a lavish gift because he's a lavish giver. And he doesn't want you to pay him back (because honestly you'd never be able to). The giving is his reward. What he does want is your heart—the same way you give your heart to your child. He wants your attention and your love and your affection. He chose you so that he could be close to you. So choose him today and tomorrow and forever.

For more, read Ephesians 1:4.

> "Even before he made the world, God loved us and chose us in Christ to be holy and without fault in his eyes" (EPHESIANS 1:4).

THE JESUS INTERRUPTION

Capture Your Gratitude

Here's a photo challenge for you to end this year of devotions: Take pictures of everything that reminds you of Jesus or that you're grateful for. Save the photos in a digital album and review them at the end of the week, asking Jesus to show you something new or insightful.

When **Stephanie Hillberry** learned as a young wife that she was infertile, she never dreamed that, 10 years later, she'd be writing a book to encourage moms. As friend and sister on the outside of motherhood looking in, she's inspired by moms: by their hard work, loving hearts, and sacrifices. This book is her gift to moms everywhere.

Where will Jesus interrupt you?

Dreaded chore...or a chance to slow down and pay attention to Jesus? When we invite Jesus to interrupt every moment of our lives—not just the quiet, tidy ones—suddenly even chores take on a whole new purpose.

For books, Bibles, devotions, planners, and coloring experiences that move Jesus into EVERY corner of your life, visit...

JesusCenteredLife.com

#JesusInterruption

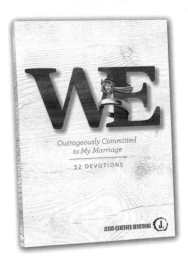

We: Outrageously Committed to My Marriage

Marriage is an epic story—complete with love, humor, and trials—lived out by courageous, flawed people.

In this book, brave husbands and wives share 52 true stories of their loving but not-so-perfect marriages. Experience renewed hope and find real wisdom as you read how Jesus brings life from the ashes of hard times, keeping love stories alive and spreading healing in the process.

You will experience...

- **Hope** as you see how Jesus shows up again and again.
- **Encouragement** as you realize you're not alone.
- **Strength** through prayer prompts that invite Jesus into your marriage in fresh ways.
- **Reflection** with journaling opportunities to record your own journey.
- **52 Devotions** that help you see how Jesus is working through your marriage to write a better story than you could ever write on your own.

To find this devotional and other Jesus-centered resources by Lifetree, visit MyLifetree.com or your favorite Christian resource provider.